"I've never mentioned it before, Leslie—but quite frankly I can see no future in this."

ANTON'S AMUSEMENT ARCADE

COLLINS
ST JAMES' PLACE · LONDON
1947

"Anton" came into being in 1937, and we—brother and sister—have been partners since then. But please don't ask us how it works out—

ANTONIA YEOMAN,

H. UNDERWOOD THOMPSON.

ACKNOWLEDGEMENTS

To the Proprietors of *Punch* for permission to reproduce drawings on pages 9-12, 14-18, 20, 22-25, 27-29, 34, 36-38, 40-42, 44-48, 50, 52, 55-57, 61-66, 68-72, 74, 76, 77, 79, 80, 83, 85-88, 90-94; to the Editor of *The Tatler and Bystander* for permission to reproduce the frontispiece and drawings on pages 26, 31-33, 35, 43, 51, 59, 60, 67, 82; to the Editor of *Lilliput* for permission to reproduce the drawing on page 78.

THIS IS A BOOK OF PICTURES ABOUT
PEOPLE WHO INHABIT A CERTAIN WORLD
WHICH MAY, OR MAY NOT, EXIST—

Perhaps it isn't a very large world—but its occupants, though not noticeably intellectual and politically somewhat unimaginative, are usually well-to-do. Mostly, of course, by inheritance—though, from time to time, some of them *can* be seen earning their directors' fees in rather prosperous-looking board-rooms while others actually do drift into such jobs as Radio Announcing, Dentistry, Lumber-jacking, Soldiering, or Inventing Secret Whatnots for the Air Ministry.

In general they are people with Tendencies.

The men, for instance, tend to have heavy eyebrows and large, black moustaches—while the women, who tend to be attractive when young, later put on weight and tend to make rather ineffectual remarks.

For the most part they live in (more or less) well-appointed houses which tend to have Picture Galleries, Libraries, a good deal of expensive Antique Furniture and Peculiar Servants. Consequently Art Exhibitions, Picture Dealers, Antique Shops, Domestic Agencies tend to be a natural part of their background.

They are social people, too. Apart from entertaining their friends in their own homes, they tend to dine out quite a bit at Expensive Restaurants, Country Pubs (and any other place where they can secure a table). They visit the Theatre, attend Banquets and occasionally Get Married.

As for recreation they go in for everything from Big-game Hunting to trying their skill at Skating, Dog Breeding and in Amusement Arcades.

While, as parents, they tend to produce fairly alert children.

They suffer the inconveniences of life fairly cheerfully. The rationing of Food, Fuel, Finance and Clothing they take in their stride.

Finally, and above all else, these people do tend to be Afflicted with Burglars.

Other types of crook—particularly forgery experts who seem to be (regrettably) influenced by the American film gangster in the matter of clothing, tend to appear from time to time—but they never displace the masked honest-to-goodness British Burglar—either at large or in captivity.

THIS IS A BOOK OF PICTURES ABOUT
PEOPLE WHO INHABIT A CERTAIN WORLD
WHICH MAY, OR MAY NOT, EXIST.

" Yes? "

"I'm afraid we have no domestic staff on our books at the moment."

"I can't think how you can be so careless, Alice—the tin was clearly
marked Trinitrotoluol."

"For instance—obviously you haven't done under THIS bed."

"AND AT SAXONE THEY MEASURE BOTH FEET"

"My husband's no good as an electrician—but he's terribly clever at carpentry."

"I was just looking for my spectacles, dear, and the ladder fell down."

"Do we wish to let our house, dear?"

"Yes—with our furniture it would look quite nice."

"I say—WHAT a crush there was in that pastel room."

"Is there a washer-up in the audience?"

" What's happened so far?"

"Mine's got the Africa Star AND the Burma Star."

"3 oz. golden syrup, 1 oz. lemonade powder, 2 oz. sherbet and 4 oz. honey and glycerine lozenges—tell me, just who made out this prescription?"

"Oh look—Michael has taught your little boy his newest game."

"I don't like the look of it, it's too easy."

"—and just think—if we adopt Mrs. Stote for our prospective candidate
we can use 'Vote for Stote' as a slogan."

"He's quite harmless except that he bites."

"Listen carefully, doctor, and I'll say ' Boom ' every
time Roger's heart beats."

31

"But what a frightful price for a hat."
"It's a frightful hat, madam."

"Aren't they little lambs?"

"That will be £1,500 for the solitaire and 9d. to cover postage and packing."

"Am I supposed to identify her—or is she supposed to identify me?"

"This may hurt a little."

"I got these from an Indian Rajah."

"Seems quite a good show at the Palladrome—what about printing a couple of tickets?"

"I hear the Government is wanting American dollars."

"Perhaps I should introduce myself—I am Detective-Sergeant Thompson of the Criminal Investigation Department."

" . . . and 20 years ago, when we was kids, we made a
tryst to meet here to-night . . ."

"Well—promise me you'll catch me if I jump."

" It's for you."

"The toughest district is round about Scotland Yard—we have to go about in pairs near there."

"I'm selling this for a friend."

"Well, then—ALL my husband's clothing coupons."

"We must have some new patches—these are so shabby."

"Fishmonger my foot—I bet you went and caught it in the river."

"Now in the next game we all go out for an hour and
come back with lumps of coal."

"And when the fire gets too hot, we just switch on the electric cooling system."

"But there's no question of petrol—I'm running on ten thousand torch batteries."

'Just mix one coupon's worth with these oats and give them to the horse."

"By Jove—how extraordinary—an African elephant in India."

"The gentleman to stuff the elephant, sir."

"On second thoughts—wasn't that rather odd?"

"I've heard there's rather a quaint local superstition about eating ' Spotted Dick ' on Midsummer Day."

63

"A Mr. Dixon of the Ministry of Supply Synthetic-Rubber Research Department would very much appreciate your recipe for 'Crêpes au Fromage.'"

"You wished to speak to the Manager, sir?—He's over in New York."

"And, above all, remember you will be employed to expedite egress—
and not just to chuck people out."

"Well, if it won't go in—it won't. 'Under the stairs' will have to remain a single room."

"Are you ready to cut the cake, Madam?"

But before our distinguished guest commences his speech, I'd like to tell you something of importance."

"I was the Chairman of the Board until I found out about the rates for overtime."

" Well, here's the last of the January jobs, Fred, No. 91 Church Street
burst pipe."

"Of course—you don't HAVE to take my advice."

"And THOSE I won at an amusement arcade for rolling
little balls through tiny little doorways marked with
different numbers."

" Hello, Joe, anything new ? "

"My husband is on nodding acquaintance with practically every auctioneer
in the town."

"I don't know if it's true, but THIS chair is said to be stuffed full
of golden sovereigns."

"You know I'm finding all sorts of things in these books
that I didn't know."

"In the family we just refer to it as Van Dyck's frolic."

"And this is my wife's little den."

" . . . and Alfred and I INSIST on having our revenge
next week."

"I always think good service should be unobtrusive, don't you?"

" Never again will I let my house furnished to a troupe of midgets."

"My idea is to cut off their retreat right here."

"And with the aid of these delicate instruments we are able to tell exactly what sort of weather we're having."

" . . . and so for your birthday I'm sending you a record of that lovely
ballad ' Trees.'"

"I admit it's interesting—but please remember we've come out here to record the song of the nightingale."